OUT OF HELL AND WONDER

Ten-Minute Plays by DogEar

DOG EAR PLAYWRIGHTS

**Kim Dunbar, Robert Fieldsteel, Katy Hickman,
Wayne Peter Liebman, Leon Martell, Jennifer Maisel,
Steve Totland, Jacqueline Wright**

Tinderbox Books
Los Angeles

Library of Congress (LCCN): 2016904980

CONTENTS

INTRODUCTION

DogEar is a collective of award-winning Los Angeles playwrights who have been conspiring to support one another's writing for over a decade.

Out of Hell and Wonder is a collection of short, variously themed plays by DogEar members. Most of these plays have been commissioned and performed in Los Angeles. For further information about the plays, and about DogEar, please visit dogear.org.

For permission to perform *Out of Hell and Wonder* or any plays therein, please contact Leon Martell (belon@ucla.edu).

Plays by DogEar members have been presented by Steppenwolf, Actors Theatre of Louisville, Woolly Mammoth, The Geffen Playhouse, Lincoln Center Director's Lab, the Hollywood Bowl, 24th Street Theatre, The Walt Disney Concert Hall, The Broad Stage, Theatre of Note, The Met Theatre, The Road, the Virginia Avenue Project, Cal Arts, Occidental College, The Ensemble Studio Theatre, Moving Arts, Sundance Theatre Lab, The O'Neill Theater Center, The Lark, The Magic Theatre, A.S.K. Theatre Projects, The Colony and many others.

Members of DogEar are Mickey Birnbaum, Bryan Davidson,

Kim Dunbar, Robert Fieldsteel, Katy Hickman, Cody Henderson, Wayne Peter Liebman, Leon Martell, Jennifer Maisel, Steve Totland, and Jacqueline Wright.

Somewhere off the coast of Mexico swims a baby sea turtle named DogEar.

GOODY FUCKING TWO SHOES

BY JENNIFER MAISEL

AUTHOR'S NOTE

Wayne Liebman's "everyone in Dog Ear should write a witch play" mandate ignited the flames of *Goody Fucking Two Shoes*, in which two high school girls fiercely vie for the lead in a *Crucible*-like school play, under the watchful eye of the drama teacher. *Goody* became a Heideman finalist at Actors Theatre of Louisville and was slated for production in the Humana Festival. However, when I originally wrote *Goody*, the play within the play was not *Crucible*-like, it was *The Crucible*, only in the short time we had, I couldn't get the rights to use the 62 words the girls quoted from Miller's play for their audition. I went back and read the 1200 pages of the original Salem witch trial manuscripts and rewrote. The school play became *Salem!*, the play itself became sharper and more poignant. *Goody* was brilliantly directed by Wendy McClellan for the apprentice showcase and for the Humana Festival, with Megan Goodchild, Deanna McGovern and Sean Dougherty in the cast. Emily Chase directed a stellar production in Los Angeles for *The Witching Hour*, with Lucy Bansley, Heather Klinke and Dameon Clarke.

— Jennifer Maisel

CAST OF CHARACTERS

ABIGAIL — 16, just beginning to understand her power over boys, over girls, over parents and teachers.

BET — 16, new, tentative, she's got to check in with Abigail that what's she's saying is cool.

MAN'S VOICE

GOODY FUCKING TWO SHOES

Music–intense, frenzied. Spotlight slams on:

ABIGAIL: "I am lost of God."

Music/lights slam up to reveal BET'S bedroom: a bed and packed boxes. ABIGAIL and BET enter. ABIGAIL glances at her script, throws it down, jumps on the bed and emotes. Overlapping slightly.

ABIGAIL: "The devil hath got hold of us."

BET: This is really nice of you, Abigail.

ABIGAIL: "The devil hath got hold of us. I gave the devil my soul and my body."

BET: I never even thought about going out for drama at my old school—it totally sucks that my parents moved me mid year. Again.

Simultaneous:

—

ABIGAIL: "I ate his red bread. I drank his wine."

BET: My dad's company says jump and he says how far would you like that transfer to go up my ass?

——

A slight grin from ABIGAIL. BET is encouraged.

BET: I told them that *this* time I'm not unpacking –

ABIGAIL flops down on the bed on her back.

ABIGAIL: *(softly, to herself)* "*The dark man* carried me. The *dark* man carried me. The dark man *carried* me"

BET: No, I'm not because I swear to God the last two times the moment I got unpacked, the moment I got comfortable, the moment I got – fucking – friends, that was it, pack it up again, Betsy –

ABIGAIL: Betsy?

BET: Yeah, I just thought here, being called Bet . . .

(ABIGAIL shrugs)

Simultaneous:

——

ABIGAIL: *(softly, to herself)* "I gave the devil my soul and my body."

BET: Betsy, Bet—you'll like this new school better, less crime, higher median test scores, a better breed of kids.

—

ABIGAIL: "I know Goody Parker to be a witch. *I* know Goody Parker to be a witch. I *know* Goody Parker to be a witch. I know–"

BET: Breed–like cattle or dogs. They don't understand that better breeds come from puppy mills and are like *(shouts out the door)* deformed in their perfection!

ABIGAIL: *(whispers)* "I know Goody Parker to be a witch."

BET: Anyway—it's really nice of you. I mean today, today was the fourth day I walked into the cafeteria and walked out in a row. I don't know, how am I supposed to know where to sit? How am I supposed to know what to order even? And carrying my tray and my books and then looking around, everyone knows when you're looking around, don't you think? And they look away, they just edge away in case you think they like you and there's someone you always think is liking you and they're really looking at the person behind you—so after-school special—and then you're caught and you think if there is a god the—fucking—building will implode right that second and then the second after that with everyone still staring at you holding the stupid tray you've gotten confirmation that there is no god at all.

So which table do you sit at?

ABIGAIL: I smoke.

BET: I should smoke. That way when my mother says to me all you have to do to make friends is take up an activity I can say I did Mom, I smoke. That was great advice Mom. Watch her vegan facelift fall flat after that.

ABIGAIL: "The devil hath got hold of us. The devil hath got hold of us. Thedevilhathgotholdofus. The. Devil. Hath. Got. Hold. Of. Us."

BET: I figured if I just get to be a screaming girl or I like work the lights or something there'd be, I don't know . . .

ABIGAIL: "The dark man carried me. He whispered in my ear." He tempted me to sing for him.

BET: "He tempted me to write in his book."

ABIGAIL: What?

BET: "The dark man carried me. He whispered in my ear. He tempted me to write in his book."

ABIGAIL: "—to write in his book?"

BET: Yeah.

ABIGAIL: Are you sure? *(Bet tosses her the script. Abigail looks.)* What the fuck does that mean?

BET: I know.

ABIGAIL: I mean I get the whole, I gave the devil my soul and my body, definitely. I get the whole ate the red bread, drank his wine, oh lord comfort me crap–I mean I can get it even though I'm a Jew-Bu–but he tempted me to write in his book? Big fucking deal.

BET: I know.

ABIGAIL: Hey, I'm Satan, don't you want to sign my yearbook? All the other kids are doing it.

BET: I know!

ABIGAIL: Fuck. I don't know why we couldn't do something good, like RENT.

BET: You should, you should tell them RENT.

ABIGAIL: But this is "historical". Culled from actual transcripts. SALEM. Exclamation point. I mean, I like Mrs. Polk—she's an OK history teacher—but she's no Jonathan Larson. She's not even Arthur Miller.

BET: *(clearly not knowing who she's talking about)* Right.

ABIGAIL: But this, god, with all the screaming, they're just screaming. We have to scream at the audition. And have fits. And Goody this and Goody that. Goody Good. Please. I know Goody Fucking Two Shoes is a witch.

BET: I know!

ABIGAIL: Craig says—

BET: Craig?

ABIGAIL: Mr. MacNamara—some of us, who are you know, close to him, he told us that we can call him that. We're not supposed to but he says respect doesn't come with a mister—

BET: Or a Goody–

ABIGAIL: What? Oh. So if like anyone else is around–you know–Maybe if your audition goes OK then you can call him—

Music/light shift slam. Two spotlights. The audition.

ABIGAIL/BET: "Oh, my heart will break within me. I am lost of God. The devil hath got hold of us. I gave the devil my soul and my body. I ate his red bread. I drank his wine. The dark man carried me. He whispered in my ear. He tempted me to write in his book. I have seen Goody Martin among the witches. I have seen Goody Proctor among the witches. Goody Cloyse and Goody Good were their deacons. Oh Goody Hoar do not kill me. She bites . . . she bites! They will tear me to pieces!!! Oh lord comfort me and bring out all that are witches!"

ABIGAIL'S light goes out.

BET: I am lost . . . of God.

Light shift slam. BET'S bedroom.

ABIGAIL: None of these girls–none of them have any backbone. They're just followers.

BET: I know exactly what you mean.

ABIGAIL: Except Abigail.

BET: Well Abigail.

ABIGAIL: She's got—

BET: I guess it's—it's . . .

ABIGAIL: It's power. She's found it. What everyone's scared of—

BET: Huh?

ABIGAIL: Teenage girls. Us. And that.

BET: What?

ABIGAIL: Power.

BET: Huh?

ABIGAIL: Why else would they care about what we wear? Why else would they talk about uniforms? Dress codes? Why else would they force us to do this play–long dresses, Goody this, Goody that, Sirs and whippings and screaming girls and God. Deciding what God says, what God wants, that couldn't—stop me—

BET: You?

ABIGAIL: Abigail.

BET: Oh, I didn't get, I just thought, you, me, Abigail, your name and hers, that's like destiny—

ABIGAIL: Meisner.

BET: What?

ABIGAIL: Sense memory. Trying to, you know, get into the part. To be the part.

BET: Wow.

ABIGAIL: What?

BET: You've got, like a technique. If you hate the play so much then why . . . ?

ABIGAIL: I'm an actress.

Light shift slam. A spotlight on each of them.

MAN'S VOICE: Whenever you're ready.

ABIGAIL and BET each let out horrific, silent screams, sinking over-dramatically into the ground.

MAN'S VOICE: Great. Let's try a little adjustment.

ABIGAIL and BET each let out horrific, silent screams, sinking over-dramatically into the ground.

MAN'S VOICE: And again

ABIGAIL and BET each let out horrific, silent screams, sinking over-dramatically into the ground.

The spotlight on BET goes out. ABIGAIL shades her eyes against the spotlight's glare.

ABIGAIL: You have got to be kidding me.

MAN'S VOICE: Don't be this way.

ABIGAIL: You have got to be fucking kidding me.

MAN'S VOICE: There's a covenant I've made, Abigail.

ABIGAIL: Jesus.

MAN'S VOICE: I have to judge each audition solely on its individual merits. I must stay in the moment. I have to rate my emotional response, my visceral reaction, my gut feeling of which character suits each auditioner best—

ABIGAIL: She's the new girl.

MAN'S VOICE: Her Abigail was quite—

ABIGAIL: So what you're saying is, past performance doesn't count, Craig.

Slam music and light shift. The two spotlights.

MAN'S VOICE: And . . . go—

ABIGAIL and BET each in their own light, each in a frenzied mad fit/dance, each transported with the music.)

The spotlight on ABIGAIL goes out.

BET: Really?

MAN'S VOICE: Quite . . . um . . . moving.

BET: So there's a chance with you for me—

MAN'S VOICE: What?

BET: For a part.

MAN'S VOICE: Oh. Oh.

BET: I was just hoping to be able to speak.   You know, on the stage . . . because these words are so . . . so . . . evocative –

She touches her collarbone, arching her back slightly—provocatively? Purposefully? Or not.

MAN'S VOICE: Oh?

Slam light and music shift.

Spotlight on ABIGAIL shading her eyes against the spotlight glare.

ABIGAIL: Past performance doesn't count. Obviously. Craig.

MAN'S VOICE: Don't—you, of all students, Abigail. You believe in the power of theatre, you wouldn't want me to break the faith–

ABIGAIL: Break the faith–

MAN'S VOICE: That the other students have that they'll be judged on their merits only, fairly–and

ABIGAIL: Craig.

MAN'S VOICE: Don't—

ABIGAIL: Don't what? Don't do this? *(She begins to unbutton her shirt.)* Maybe I need to audition again.

Spotlight on BET as well.

ABIGAIL/BET: "Oh my heart will break within me. I am lost of God."

Simultaneous

———

ABIGAIL: "The devil hath got hold of us"

BET: It's so simple. It's so what I feel right now.

———

ABIGAIL unbuttons her shirt. ABIGAIL touches herself

BET: I feel so lost. Of everything. Of everyone . . . If I could get over that feeling of being watched, of–

ABIGAIL: I gave the devil my soul–and my body.

BET: needing, of needing, of wanting just for someone to give me the–the–do you understand? Somehow, I think you

Spotlight on BET

BET: Somehow I think you could help me . . . find myself.

MAN'S VOICE: *(hoarse)* Find yourself?

BET: You know . . . as my director—

Light slam—spotlight on ABIGAIL.

ABIGAIL: "The devil hath got hold of us." –That's pretty accurate, don't you think?

MAN'S VOICE: What are you—

ABIGAIL: "The devil hath got hold of me. I gave the devil my soul . . . and my body."

MAN'S VOICE: What?

ABIGAIL: Wouldn't the faculty be stunned to hear that?

MAN'S VOICE: Abigail—

ABIGAIL: Wouldn't want it to get to the PTA. Did you know I'm editor of the paper?

BET'S spotlight turns on.

BET: "I am lost."

MAN'S VOICE: Nothing happened.

ABIGAIL: Are you sure? There are different ways to touch, you know? There are different way to interact. After all, who controls that spotlight? I know the warmth is coming from you. I know the heat that is coming from you.

MAN'S VOICE: You . . . you wouldn't.

ABIGAIL: I felt his hands. I felt the warmth. I felt the heat. I felt it penetrate me and I couldn't look at him. I couldn't look at him in the eyes. He wouldn't let me. *(She stands, shirt unbuttoned.)* You know there's a bunch of kids still waiting in the hall for their callbacks. Maybe I should go.

MAN'S VOICE: Abigail.

ABIGAIL: Yes. Craig?

MAN'S VOICE: You're . . . Abigail.

BET: "I am lost."

ABIGAIL: See you at rehearsal, Mr. MacNamara. *(She walks off the stage.)*

BET: "I am lost."

MAN'S VOICE: Thank you–that was very . . . nice.

BET beams at him.

END OF PLAY

FACE VALUE

---

by Steve Totland

AUTHOR'S NOTE

Face Value was named a finalist for Actors Theatre of Louisville's Heideman Award. The play was first produced at 24th Street Theatre, in Los Angeles, as part of an evening of plays entitled *Chatter*. That production was directed by Meighan Gerachis. Carolyn Almos played Miranda; Rod McLachlan played Aaron; John Neisler played Robert.

— Steve Totland

CAST OF CHARACTERS

MIRANDA — Female; mid-30s to late-50s.

AARON — Male; mid-30s to late-50s

ROBERT — Male; mid-30s to late-50s.

Miranda and Robert are husband and wife.

FACE VALUE

The dining room of AARON'S house. The last bits of a good meal lie scattered on the dining room table.

ROBERT and AARON sit at the table. MIRANDA stands next to AARON. She peers, intently, into AARON'S face.

MIRANDA: I don't see a thing. You've had them how long?

AARON: About a month.

MIRANDA: Really? (*She scrutinizes his face. Steps back. To ROBERT.*) Maybe you—

ROBERT stands as MIRANDA sits.

ROBERT: Where did you say—

AARON: Under my eye.

ROBERT leans in for a closer look.

ROBERT: Your right eye?

AARON: My right eye. Then, over by my nose.

ROBERT: And it's what that I'm looking for?

ARRON: Bumps.

ROBERT: Mmm.

AARON: Little bumps that are, slightly, red.

ROBERT: Slightly red bumps.

ROBERT examines AARON'S face.

AARON: You see anything?

ROBERT: No.

AARON: You're sure?

ROBERT: You want the truth?

AARON: I do. I want the truth.

ROBERT: You've got a blackhead—

MIRANDA: (*Throwing her napkin at ROBERT.*) That's disgusting.

ROBERT: (*Catching her throw.*) –and a couple of humongous nose hairs. But no bumps.

The men share a laugh.

MIRANDA: (*Standing.*) You are so rude.

MIRANDA begins clearing the table.

AARON: You don't have to do that.

MIRANDA: You made the meal—

AARON: After you've had me for dinner how many times?

MIRANDA: That's what friends do.

AARON: That's what good friends do. It doesn't take much and you learn pretty quickly who your good friends really are.

MIRANDA: Well. . . I would say people who are not good friends are not really friends at all. They're acquaintances. (*To ROBERT.*) Isn't that how you see it?

ROBERT nods his head "Yes."

MIRANDA gives AARON a warm smile.

After a prolonged moment.

AARON: That was maudlin. I'm sorry—

MIRANDA: There's nothing to be sorry—

AARON: (*Overlapping MIRANDA.*) That was not on the agenda. (*Taking the plates from MIRANDA.*) Sit. And relax.

MIRANDA sits.

AARON gathers plates.

MIRANDA motions to ROBERT.

ROBERT gathers plates.

AARON: Either of you want coffee? Or tea? (*Seeing ROBERT holding plates.*) Put those down. This is my treat.

ROBERT sets down the plates. He sits.

MIRANDA: I'll have coffee.

ROBERT: You have tea?

AARON: You want black, or herbal?

MIRANDA: You know what? I'll have tea. Don't make a pot of coffee—

AARON: I'm having coffee. Decaf?

MIRANDA: Decaf's great.

AARON looks to ROBERT.

ROBERT: You have some of that mint?

AARON: Mint it is.

AARON disappears into the kitchen, his hands full of dishes.

MIRANDA: So?

ROBERT is unsure what she means.

MIRANDA: Did you see bumps?

ROBERT: No. Did you?

MIRANDA: No.

ROBERT: Then, why are you asking?

MIRANDA: No reason. I just—

ROBERT: You think I saw bumps, but said I didn't?

MIRANDA: No.

ROBERT: Why would I lie? What would be the point of that?

MIRANDA: To save his feelings?

ROBERT: Save his feelings? A friend thinks he has bumps, you have an obligation to speak the truth.

MIRANDA is silent.

ROBERT: You saw bumps?

MIRANDA: Did I say I saw bumps? If Aaron has bumps we would see them. They would be on his face. Plain as day.

AARON enters with a plate of fancy cookies and colorful napkins.

AARON: It'll be just another minute for the hot things.

AARON, sensing he's interrupted something, gazes at MIRANDA and ROBERT.

After a moment,

MIRANDA: (*The cookies.*) They're so beautiful.

AARON sets down the plate, then passes out napkins.

AARON: I got them at Angeline's.

Each takes a cookie.

They eat.

AARON: What you said about blackheads reminds me. My aunt lived next door to this woman who had this thing on her face. It looked like a blackhead. Only she couldn't get rid of it. She squeezed. It wouldn't go away. But, it didn't bother her. So she, ultimately, didn't think much about it. But, then, one day, it got bigger. And it started to hurt. And, all the sudden, I think she was in church, my aunt said the blackhead popped open. And it was full of spiders. It wasn't a blackhead at all. A spider had laid eggs in her face. And they hatched. But, because she was in church, she didn't scream. Or, leave. She was afraid people would think she was dirty if they knew a spider laid eggs in her face. So, she just sat there. And, the spiders crawled all over her face. And they bit her. Some of them in her eyes. And, they were black widow spiders. And, she died.

ROBERT: Uh-huh.

AARON: You don't believe me? You can ask my Aunt Ruth. You want me to get her number?

From off, the whistle of a tea kettle.

AARON stands.

ROBERT: Aaron.

AARON: You can choose to not believe me.

MIRANDA: No one said they don't believe you.

ROBERT: In fact, I was just about to say the same thing happened to my cousin. Only, with her, they were ants. And, because she has cancer, they weren't in her face. They were in her wig.

AARON gives ROBERT a long look straight in the eyes.

AARON: Talk to Aunt Ruth. She'll tell you it happened.

AARON goes into the kitchen.

MIRANDA: You are amazing.

ROBERT: What?

MIRANDA: Teasing him. Your best friend is sitting here; telling us this story—

ROBERT: Which he has to know we know is made up.

MIRANDA: Yes.

ROBERT: "Call my Aunt." What is that? He's daring me to call?

MIRANDA: He knows you won't call. Believing him is not the point. It's like with the bumps. It's his way of saying, "Look at me. I need someone to notice me." It's a cry for help.

ROBERT: People have tried. He pushes them away. (Standing.) Let's not stay too long.

ROBERT kisses MIRANDA, then heads for the hallway.

MIRANDA: Where are you going?

ROBERT: To pee.

ROBERT exits.

AARON reenters. He carries coffee and tea service on a tray.

AARON: Here we are. Where's Robert?

MIRANDA: He's in the little boys. Listen—

As AARON lays out the hot drinks.

MIRANDA: —your bumps . . . Do they hurt?

AARON, grateful for a chance to speak about his affliction, sits.

AARON: Not really. Sometimes they're a little warm. Like a small sunburn. It looks bad, don't you think?

MIRANDA: No. If you hadn't said something I wouldn't have even noticed.

AARON: You saw them?

MIRANDA nods her head, "Yes."

AARON: You said you didn't.

MIRANDA: I know.

AARON: Both of you. You said you didn't see them.

MIRANDA: We were embarrassed.

AARON: You talked behind my back?

MIRANDA: We were caught off guard. I'm sorry. We didn't know what to say.

AARON: (*Empathetic.*) That's how it is. People at my new job are totally unwilling to acknowledge . . .

AARON is unable to continue.

MIRANDA leans across the table. She takes his hand.

ROBERT returns. He stops, surprised by what he sees.

AARON sees ROBERT, pulls himself together.

AARON: (*To Robert.*) Here's your tea. I forget if you like lemon.

ROBERT: Just a little sugar.

AARON: If it's cold I can nuke it—

ROBERT: (*Testing the temperature.*) This is great.

MIRANDA: (*To Robert.*) I fessed up. I told Aaron we saw the bumps.

ROBERT: Ah!

AARON: You shouldn't be embarrassed. I'm not. I'm the one that asked you to look.

ROBERT: Yes.

AARON: I'm worried. I'm nervous. It's hard for me to, sometimes, concentrate. But, I'm not embarrassed.

MIRANDA: What does the doctor say?

AARON: That's what's so frustrating. The good dermatologists are all booked. My internist would squeeze me in. But he's just going to say I need to see a specialist.

MIRANDA: You should see a doctor.

AARON: I am. Just not for another three weeks. By then, I'll be The Elephant Man.

ROBERT stands.

ROBERT: (*To MIRANDA.*) It's getting late.

MIRANDA: (*Surprised. Setting down her coffee.*) Oh—

AARON: You're not going, are you?

ROBERT: I have work tomorrow. I've got a huge project—

AARON: It seems like you just got here—

ROBERT: You get yourself in a state. You trick yourself, and everyone around you, into believing you're the victim of a crime, or some injustice—

AARON: Did I say I was a victim?

ROBERT: It's not going to work. Not this time. We are not going to twist ourselves into knots. Wrapped around your little finger. Thinking you have cancer—

AARON: Cancer?

ROBERT: Which is what you want.

AARON: Who said cancer?

ROBERT: You want us to feel responsible—

AARON: I asked about bumps. "I think I have bumps—"

ROBERT: You lost your job and your girlfriend left. Okay. Look. The job . . . You're right. That was wrong. You'd worked there a long time. You were a good employee. They're bastards for letting you go and they should all rot in hell. But, Laurie was a bitch. You knew it. I knew it. She knew it. Everyone knew it.

She picked a hell-of-a-time to go but, you know what? It was inevitable. The two of you would never have worked. So, here's the thing.

MIRANDA: Robby, maybe, you ought to—

ROBERT: (*To MIRANDA.*) No. (*To AARON.*) Here's the thing. Bad things happens. They do. They happen all the time. They don't mean you're a loser. They don't mean you're special. And they don't mean you're dying.

AARON: (*To MIRANDA.*) Shall I wrap up some roast beef—

MIRANDA nods her head, "No." She stands.

ROBERT: And what's with this, "I have an aunt who has a friend?" "You can call my Aunt Ruth." Your Aunt Ruth is dead. I went to her funeral.

MIRANDA: It was a lovely dinner. I had a really . . .

MIRANDA leaves.

ROBERT: Did you hear what I said?

AARON: My face does not lie. You look at my face and you know, whatever it is I'm saying, I am speaking the truth. My Mom and Dad, the entire time I was growing up, that's what they said. "Aaron has a face that cannot lie." I have bumps. And they're spreading. Something is happening to me, and it's out of control, and it's registering on my face.

ROBERT leaves.

AARON alone.

He touches his face along the cheekbones; under his right eyes; under his left eye. He lets out a big, oversized sigh.

END OF PLAY

1331

by Kim Dunbar

AUTHOR'S NOTE

I had the great fortune to work with Leigh Curran, (founder and former Artistic Director of The Virginia Avenue Project), at an A.S.K. theater workshop at U.C.L.A. The Project is a free program in Los Angeles, that uses performing arts and mentoring "to help kids think creatively, critically and courageously about life goals and choices". Leigh later invited me to write a short one-act play for VAP's One-On-One Program. A child is paired with an adult writer/actor, or as in my case, with a writer and an actor. We were also encouraged to write a song into the play. Before I started a draft, I interviewed the young teen girl I was paired with, and tried to pick up on some things that interested her. Music, a fantasy trip to Hawaii, and the joy of surfing the internet stood out. I thought back about myself at her age and what I was doing. During some rough patches, I ran away from home a couple of times. Usually back with Mom within a day or so, and well fed by my Aunt and Uncle. But, there was one time when I hitched a ride in a stranger's car, and ended up in a scary situation. I realized that no one in the world knew where I was. The Secret came out of that experience, merged with the brief and possibly intuitive glimpse into the life of my young artist. The process was unique and thought provoking. I learned given the opportunity, young people often have the innate ability to handle mature material in a way that rings deep and true.

— Kim Dunbar

CAST OF CHARACTERS

GIRL — Age 13

OTHER GIRL — Age 13 and 31

1331

A bus stop bench, plastered with photos of a young teen girl, "HAVE YOU SEEN ME?" in captions underneath. Newspapers cover a person lying on the bench. GIRL enters, dragging a large duffle bag. She looks down the street for the bus, then sticks out her thumb to hitch a ride.

A moment later, a car horn honks loudly.

OTHER GIRL bolts up from under the newspapers, startling GIRL. OTHER GIRL wears an old pair of boots, her clothes are ripped in places and look way too small. She yawns and stretches awake, then looks over at GIRL.

Honk!

OTHER GIRL: You know him?

GIRL: No.

OTHER GIRL: I think he's waiting for you.

GIRL: Yeah . . . I don't like Toyotas.

OTHER GIRL: Why not?

GIRL: 'Cause everybody's got 'em.

OTHER GIRL looks back in the direction of the car.

OTHER GIRL: It's a nice shade of red. Look, he's waving. You should go.

GIRL: *(yells to driver)* No, thank you! Sorry! *(to OTHER GIRL)* I'll wait for another one.

OTHER GIRL: Your loss. Wanna hula hoop?

She pulls a pink hula hoop out from under the bus stop bench, and gets it going around her waist.

GIRL: You're pretty good.

OTHER GIRL: Been practicing a LONG time. Wanna try?

GIRL: That's okay.

OTHER GIRL: C'mon!

GIRL takes the hula hoop from her and gives it a go.

OTHER GIRL: You almost got it. Faster! GO!!

The hula hoop falls to the ground. GIRL steps out of it and hands it back.

GIRL: You're better. How old are you?

OTHER GIRL: That depends.

GIRL: You have fake ID?

OTHER GIRL: No. Sometimes there's more than one answer to a question. No, really. What color are my eyes?

GIRL leans in to look.

GIRL: Brown.

OTHER GIRL: Not always. Depends on what I'm wearing. Like, whenever I wear red, my eyes are always bloodshot.

GIRL: Uh, huh. So—how old are you?

OTHER GIRL: Thirty-one.

GIRL: Right.

OTHER GIRL: Thirteen.

GIRL: You don't look thirteen. Or thirty-one. Definitely can't be both.

OTHER GIRL: Can too.

GIRL: Can not.

OTHER GIRL: Can too!

GIRL: Not!

OTHER GIRL: TOO!

GIRL: PROVE IT!!

OTHER GIRL: Guess that means you don't take my word for it? Okay. Okay. Well, to understand, first you have to know I'm famous.

GIRL: You are? What movies have you been in?

OTHER GIRL: I don't do movies.

GIRL: Then what are you famous for?

OTHER GIRL: I can't tell you.

GIRL: Are you a singer?

OTHER GIRL: Nope.

GIRL: Athlete?

OTHER GIRL: Unh uh.

GIRL: Politician? Talk show host? Race car driver, reality show contestant, royalty . . . murderer??

OTHER GIRL shakes her head "no" to all.

GIRL: You're not a writer.

OTHER GIRL: Hell to the naw!

GIRL: This is getting annoying. Why don't you just tell me?

OTHER GIRL: It's a secret.

GIRL: I'm good at secrets. I won't tell anyone.

OTHER GIRL: Most people don't keep secrets. They give 'em away like Easter bunnies.

GIRL: What if I tell you one about me, then you tell me yours?

OTHER GIRL: My secret's a BIG one. Yours gotta be the same size.

GIRL: Well . . . I'm going to Hawaii. Like, right now.

OTHER GIRL: No way.

GIRL: Got all my stuff in this bag.

OTHER GIRL: Wow. That's a long swim.

GIRL: I'm flying.

OTHER GIRL: With those arms—I don't think so.

GIRL: On a plane!

OTHER GIRL: Yeah? Let's see your ticket.

GIRL: My friend has it. I'm going to pick it up now but he lives kind of far.

OTHER GIRL: Must be a really good friend to buy you a ticket to Hawaii. Where'd you meet him?

GIRL: Online. His screen name is GoodieMan.

OTHER GIRL: GoodieMan?

GIRL: Kinda lame I know, but he's so cool. When I told him I always wanted to go to bungee jumping in Hawaii, he said he'd buy me a ticket for my birthday. He's awesome.

OTHER GIRL: Today's your birthday?

GIRL: Yup. Fourteen.

OTHER GIRL: Fourteen. Lucky you. Happy birthday.

GIRL: Thanks.

OTHER GIRL: What do Mom and Dad think about GoodieMan?

GIRL shrugs.

OTHER GIRL: Didn't tell them, did ya?

GIRL: Nope.

OTHER GIRL: Slick! They won't hear it from me.

She zips her mouth shut and throws away the key.

GIRL: I can't wait. *(beat)* You'd go, right? If you were in my shoes?

OTHER GIRL: Most def. Sounds like the trip of a lifetime.

A car honks. GIRL looks up the street and sees the car.

GIRL: It's a BMW! Yes!

OTHER GIRL: So predictable.

GIRL: I love Beemers. Especially silver ones.

GIRL grabs her duffle bag.

OTHER GIRL: Looks like his license plate fell off . . .

GIRL: See you later.

OTHER GIRL: Nice knowin' you. For five minutes.

GIRL: Me too. You're the best hula hooper I've ever seen.

A longer Honk! GIRL heads for the car.

OTHER GIRL: Have fun in Hawaii. *(beat)* Wait!

GIRL *stops and looks back at OTHER GIRL.*

OTHER GIRL: Don't you want to know why I'm famous? And two ages at the same time?

GIRL: Yeah, but . . .

She looks toward the car, then back at OTHER GIRL.

OTHER GIRL: You asked . . .

GIRL: *(to car)* Never mind! Sorry! *(to OTHER GIRL)* Guess there'll be another one.

OTHER GIRL: There's always another one.

GIRL: Okay. So, what are you famous for and how can you be two ages at the same time?

OTHER GIRL: Promise you won't judge me?

GIRL: Promise.

OTHER GIRL: 'Cause until you've been in my shoes . . . in fact . . . you need to be in my shoes, I mean my boots! To know what I'm talking about. What size are you?

GIRL: Seven and a half.

OTHER GIRL: Me too! Perfect! Let's switch.

GIRL takes off her shoes and hands them to OTHER GIRL. OTHER GIRL takes off her boots and hands them to GIRL. Suddenly, the smell hits GIRL like a ton of bricks.

GIRL: Ohhh ... ugh ... peeewwwwwww ... !!!

GIRL is almost ready to puke.

OTHER GIRL: What's wrong with you?

GIRL: Your . . . boots . . . they . . . really really . . . REALLY STINK!

OTHER GIRL: Yours don't smell like no rose garden neither.

GIRL: NO. This is the WORST thing I've ever smelled in my life. UGH! Why do they smell so BAD?

OTHER GIRL: Humph. You really want to know?

GIRL shakes her head "yes".

Music cue. They sing the following:

OTHER GIRL: I, like you, wanted to run away

GIRL: Run away

OTHER GIRL: I, like you, thought things were bad

GIRL: Oh, so bad

OTHER GIRL: I like you, thought the answer to all

that was wrong in my life

could be pushed right aside

GIRL: You, like me, thought you could run away

OTHER GIRL: Run away

GIRL: You, like me, thought things were bad

OTHER GIRL: Oh, so bad

GIRL: You, like me, thought the answer to all

that was wrong in your life

could be pushed right aside

OTHER GIRL: Then I left home,

on that morning in May

A neighbor said he saw me,

GIRL: Saw you headin' that way

OTHER GIRL: The police searched the area,

while my mother cried

GIRL: But as time crept on by,

they all thought you . . . died

Now I know, that you did run away

OTHER GIRL: I ran away

GIRL: Now, I know, why you are sad

OTHER GIRL: Oh so sad

GIRL: Now, I know that you are famous

your photo on the bus stop I've seen,

it says . . .

GIRL turns and sees the photos of OTHER GIRL on the bus bench.

OTHER GIRL: Have—you—seen—me?

Song ends. OTHER GIRL tries not to cry.

OTHER GIRL: This guy . . . he picked me up in his car . . . Ha, it was a Honda! But when I tried to get out . . . he wouldn't let me. It was my birthday. I would have been thirteen. Today. And thirty-one. Told you.

GIRL: What do you mean—would have been? You escaped. You got away from him. You can go home to your family now.

OTHER GIRL: I can't. Ever.

GIRL: *(really shaken)* You can use my cell phone . . .

OTHER GIRL: Why you think my boots smell so rotten?

GIRL: You mean . . . you're . . .

OTHER GIRL: Don't.

GIRL looks down at the boots, then quickly tosses them away.

GIRL: Sorry, it's just that—

OTHER GIRL: —Got it. You don't wanna to be in my shoes.

GIRL: It's getting late. I—I have to go.

OTHER GIRL: What about Hawaii?

GIRL: I have a softball game tomorrow. If I don't show up, I let my whole team down. My aunt's house isn't far.

OTHER GIRL: You weren't thinkin' about the team five minutes ago.

GIRL picks up her duffle and starts to leave. Then—

GIRL: Why did you tell me you would go with him? If you were in my shoes.

OTHER GIRL: Sometimes there's more than one answer to a question.

GIRL: Why?

OTHER GIRL: 'Cause I was lonely. 'Cause you get to be fourteen.

GIRL: *(beat. She sings)* Happy Birthday to you, happy birthday to you . . .

OTHER GIRL: *(sings)* Happy Birthday, happy birthday . . .

GIRL leaves.

Lights fade out.

END OF PLAY

ESSENTIAL MAGICK

by Robert Fieldsteel

AUTHOR'S NOTE

Very early on in Dog Ear's existence, Wayne Liebman suggested that all members write plays about witches. Essential Magick is the result of that challenge. Recently, I had known two Goth teenage girls who self-mutilated. They said that when they cut themselves, it was something that they had to do, it wasn't a choice, it wasn't to be cool, whatever was going on inside of them had to be released by the cutting. I thought that that kind of intensity might be well-suited to a witch play. And humoring the idea that the cutting wasn't self-destructive but, in its own way, was an act of healing, of survival, made it all the more intriguing to me. So I decided that my witch would be a young teenage girl who practiced contemporary withchery/wicca and who also had the pain and intensity to self-mutilate.

Then I thought, How would the girl's mother feel about all of this?—Especially a mother who hasn't had any children before, who's new to parenting. And it pretty much took off from there. These two women may not be in the same room, but they are powerfully connected. As dark as the play gets, I ultimately feel that the two of them will get through all of this okay. I often don't feel that way about the characters I write.

Essential Magick was produced at the MET Theatre in Los Angeles, September—October, 2005 as part of Dog Ear

Playwrights' The Witching Hour. Melina Bielefelt played Claudia and Dawn Worrell played Breanna. The play was directed by the author.

— Robert Fieldsteel

CAST OF CHARACTERS

CLAUDIA — late 30s-early 40s

BREANNA — Claudia's daughter, age 13

ESSENTIAL MAGICK

A suburban home, present day. BREANNA is in her bedroom, CLAUDIA is in the "breakfast nook" area of a kitchen. The stage may be virtually bare, although a small night table with drawers is suggested for Breanna's "room." More set elements may be used to suggest other aspects of these rooms if desired, but the preference should be for enough openness on the set to allow for the feeling of a flow of energy from actor to actor.

CLAUDIA: I still think it's good that she has her own room. But I worry. I know I can be prone to worry. But since she's become a witch, I do worry about her having her own room. It's not so much the witch part, I mean, her being a witch, that's my . . . area of concern. I know that sounds strange, but, at least the way she explains it to me, a twenty-first century witch is relatively benevolent. I mean, nobody's cackling over a cauldron or anything. It's more a worship of the "aliveness" of nature. In everything. In the world. *(beat)* I know she'd say I'm not expressing it very well. But I think I've got the general gist. No, it's, it's not the witch stuff so much as all the time she's been spending alone in her room. With the door shut. Since around the time she became a witch. Jim says that's typical for a thirteen year old. But he doesn't know about the cutting. The cuts. I don't know why I haven't told him. One day, we had a little heat spell and he asked her why she was wearing long sleeves and she said, "Have you ever seen a witch with short sleeves?" and he laughed. *(beat)* The cuts have been going on for a while. Since before she became a witch. So they're not, y'know, part and parcel. *(beat)* I remember a joke she liked, it was written on one of those wax dixie cups at her Halloween party when she was . . . nine. I still remember what the cup looked like, it was purple and there was this jack o' lantern with a skinny little body and he's talking to this witch, this kind of plump witch with green skin, and he asks, "What happened when the little witches ate all their witchtable soup?" And then you turn the cup, and he says, "They gruesome." And you see the witch's reaction, she's like: (*CLAUDIA throws up her hands and puts on a horrified expression, cartoon style*) And Breanna . . . Breanna . . . just kept giggling. And saying, "That's so stupid." *(beat)* "That's so *stupid*, I love it." *(beat)* That was four years ago. Not even. *(beat)* Sometimes I go for hours thinking of nothing but her. The day slips by.

Lights up on BREANNA. Her speech is racing. Periodically throughout, she bangs her fist[s] on the floor, on her knees, etc.

BREANNA: So I asked David for a salt packet, a lousy salt packet, he had a bunch of them on his tray and I didn't want to go all the way up to the front, maybe lose my seat, I really did want the salt packet, a couple, it's not like we're strangers and that fucking Jessica—(*bangs her fist on the floor*)—it's like a fucking fishbowl you can't do anything and I was so stupid to ask him, to sit there, I was stupid, I ask for a salt packet and she says, (*in a mocking voice*) "Oh Davey, please give me . . . " (*pause—it's painful to get the words out*) "Please give me . . . " (*bangs the floor*) " . . . give me your crumbs." (*She hits herself.*) Stupid, stupid, stupid, stupid, stupid. Why did I sit there, why did I sit there? (*beat*) I could feel him across the table, I could feel him without touching, feel his skin against me again, our skin together, our skin is meant to be together, he treats me like a stranger, he gave me the salt like a stranger in public but I felt his skin against mine across the table with our clothes on I can still feel him and I know he has to feel mine, he has to feel mine again, he didn't have to give me the salt packet, that's why he didn't look at me, he couldn't look at me, because he felt us together, naked, across the table, if you gave a packet of salt to a stranger, you'd look at them, you'd say something, "Here," you'd say, but he felt me, melting into him, and I didn't leave, I didn't leave, I couldn't leave, I sprinkled the salt on the green beans and I tasted him and I heard them giggling, not him, the others, they giggled and I tasted him in the salt and they sounded so far away. I have to see the magick. I have to see the magick in it all. I'll die if I don't. I will die. They all want to calm me and they want to kill me. They'll kill me. I can't be calm. Not their calm. I can only be part of the all. Or I'll die. It's crazy to listen to them.

Beat

CLAUDIA: Sometimes I find her embarrassing. And then I hate myself for that. I see her as a reflection of me and I shouldn't. No, that's not it, that's not it. She *is* a reflection of me. In some way. I'm her mother, for chrissake. I just shouldn't be embarrassed by her. Period. (*beat*) I wish she was happier. Teens are very intense, I was very intense, if I look back, if I think back, if I feel back, I can feel back, it wasn't that long ago. Like all these different ethers and potions are pouring around inside of you, I'm not just talking raging hormones, I can remember sitting in class and feeling a blackness wrap around my brain like hot tar and I didn't even know why. No reason. And then, then, uh, conversely, conversely, coming out of class, another class, a teacher I had a kind of a crush on, he praised a paper of mine, I still remember, it was about the plumbing systems of the ancient Mayans, and the effect, the effect of indoor running water on their culture, and he said, "This is the product of a deep and probing mind." And I came out of that class and ran down the hall and kicked my feet up, way up on the wall so that I could see the footprints up there every day until I graduated. (*beat*) I just wish she had more friends. The last person she's going to listen to is her mother. I asked her, "Don't witches belong to covens?" and she says, "Some do and some don't" and shuts her door. And then I realize that I am actually wishing that my thirteen year old daughter would join a nice coven. I mean, it's amazing where life can take you. This is not what I would have predicted for myself. Sometimes I think that that, y'know, wanting my daughter to join a nice coven is due to some amazing growth process on my part. And then sometimes I think I've lowered my standards so much that it's finally come to this.

BREANNA: They say to me things that they don't know—she, especially, the one downstairs, she thinks it's cute, she says, "Maybe you'll meet a nice Warlock" and I say, "Warlock means 'traitor,' Warlock means 'oath-breaker,' literally, look it up, mother, educate yourself, there are no nice Warlocks, the nice boys are witches, they're male witches, wrap your brain around that one." And then I say, "I've known a Warlock, mother, I've known a Warlock very well," and as the words come out I know I'm wrong, I know this is where I'm fucking up because I know I drove him away. We found the witches magick, we found it together, "essential energy," "essential energy" they call it, not the other "they" but our "they," "they"-the-wise, of the energy that flows from the gods to the humans to the vines to the rocks and we brought it to each other and inside me, him inside me, the incredible energy of us, from inside and out, from solid to liquid to air to all, not just me, so beyond me, and they, the other they, the common they, they say that boys just . . . (*bangs her fist*) . . . they just . . . (*bangs her fist*) . . . they just . . .

BREANNA continues to bang her fist.

CLAUDIA: I read about a girl, a teenage girl in Vermont who killed her mother. With knives. I don't picture that happening in Vermont. Vermont's always seemed so peaceful. The last of the 50 states to open a Walmart.

BREANNA: . . . they just *leave.* (*pause*) And that . . . explanation . . . is so *small.* He couldn't just leave because he's a part of *us* and *I* didn't leave.

CLAUDIA: The policeman asked her how she could hate her mother so much. And she said, "I don't hate my mother. I love my mother. I wanted her to feel. I wanted to give her the greatest moment of her life."

During the following, BREANNA goes to a night table, opens a drawer, takes out a small box, and removes a pair of curved cuticle scissors.

BREANNA: They say it wasn't because of me, but I know it was me. I drove him away. Because of the need. Because it was smaller than us. And that hurt him. And he went away. That's why.

CLAUDIA: And I keep picturing it in my mind. I saw her picture, the girl. She looked like a little girl. And the mother, I don't see her face, I see her torso and limbs. And they're in a woodsy kind of kitchen, homey, but dark. With a butcher block in the middle. A worn, wood butcher block.

BREANNA: I was stupid . . . (*She slashes the cuticle scissor in a straight line across her arm. CLAUDIA sits upright.*) . . . and selfish . . . and needy . . . (*another slash*) . . . and small . . .

BREANNA continues to slash herself–not constantly–she may rest at times, then start again–throughout the following:

CLAUDIA: I see the knife, a long knife, slash into her, the woman, into her waist. And again across her chest. And the top of her body, it opens up, it falls back, against the butcher block, exposing the muscle beneath, like slicing into a ripe, tropical fruit. And the woman's eyes, I see her eyes open wide, they're azure and the whites are veined like marble but I don't see her face. And the flesh, and the meat, the dark, red meat beneath the flesh, it's oddly beautiful. The muscles move, they twitch and they squirm and they flow into each other beneath that pale, pale flesh, it's like picking up a rock and finding shiny red bugs swarming beneath, beautiful and horrible and so terribly alive. And the force, the energy of that knife, the first time I imagined this, I couldn't be the girl, I could only be the mother and that frightened me because it was not because I'm a mother but because of who I am, I knew that was why, and that frightened me. And I pictured it again, and again, and again, I kept being drawn back to it, and more and more I felt myself as the little girl, going with the force of that knife, slicing into the mother again and again and I couldn't help but think . . . I know this is awful, but I couldn't help myself from thinking . . . what a remarkable little girl. That she didn't turn on herself. I know that's sick but . . . Breanna . . . I feel so helpless.

Silence. BREANNA is finished slashing.

BREANNA: I am still . . . a part of the energy of the all . . . despite my shortcomings . . . and I will touch goodness in my life and bring goodness to life around me.

CLAUDIA: I mean, I know, in real life, there's a happy medium. It's not that I don't know that that little girl wasn't . . . as misguided as can possibly be . . . but several times in the article they referred to her, the experts referred to her, as "disconnected." And that didn't seem right.

During the following, BREANNA goes back to the night table and, from another drawer, takes out some powders and liquids. And what appears to be a kind of scrapbook. Almost with a sense of a weight having been lifted, her humor more good-natured than creepy, she mutters to herself:

BREANNA: "Are you a good witch or a bad witch?" Hee-hee-hee. "Oh, I'm a good witch." I am. I yamIyamIyam.

CLAUDIA: People call me a "soccer mom." *That* seems disconnected.

BREANNA: "Fur and feathers, scales and skin, Different without but the same within."

CLAUDIA: It's not a question of . . . morality. I mean, it's obvious what she did was wrong.

BREANNA: "Crone and sage, crone and sage, wisdom is a gift of age."

CLAUDIA: But I think . . . if I can see what that little girl did . . . and still feel love for her, see in some way that she wasn't, you know, just evil . . .

BREANNA lays the powders, liquids, and scrapbook in front of her, then squeezes some blood from her arm and paints it onto her face.

BREANNA: Waste not, want not. Hey kids, join the recycling drive.

CLAUDIA: Because I *can* go there. In some way. In my mind. I may not like to. But there is a part of me . . . that keeps coming back to it.

BREANNA: *(chanting softly)* Lady weave your circle light, Fill us with your holy light, earth, air, fire, and water, Bind us to you."

CLAUDIA: Birth, you know, obstetrics, in the hospital, they try to make everything sterile.

BREANNA: "Oh Great Spirit, Earth, Sun, Sky, and Sea, You are inside and all around me."

CLAUDIA: And I was all for that. No crunchy granola clinic for me, I was into *clean.*

BREANNA: "Oh Holy Mother, Earth, Moon, and Sea . . . "

CLAUDIA: But when I got there, you know, they try to prepare you, but you feel this pain, this pain of your body, stretching so far *beyond.*

BREANNA: "You are inside and all around me."

CLAUDIA: I didn't even want them to mop me—gauze and suction, away, away. The blood was warm and it bathed me as I screamed bloody murder.

BREANNA: "Air I am, Fire I am . . . "

CLAUDIA: Screamed in the fourth hour, eighth hour, twelfth hour . . .

BREANNA: "Water, earth, and spirit I am . . . "

CLAUDIA: And only the human, the human head . . .

BREANNA: "Breeze I am, Sun I am . . . "

CLAUDIA: Casing the brain, the bloated brain . . .

BREANNA: "Brook, Mountain, and Goddess I am . . . "

CLAUDIA: Too big, too big for what we're built to be . . .

BREANNA: "Maiden I am . . . "

CLAUDIA: Slice me open, that's what they wanted, to yank her out . . .

BREANNA: "Mother I am . . . "

CLAUDIA: But I screamed and pushed and shat and pissed and bled . . .

BREANNA: "Sister, lover, crone I am."

(*Beat*)

CLAUDIA: And then I heard a wail, the first wail of life and they lifted her, bathed in blood . . .

BREANNA: (*another chant, quickly, almost whispering*) "Deep in my bone, the Goddess is alive, Deep in my blood, the life force is strong . . . "

CLAUDIA: . . . the cord uncut . . .

BREANNA: "Deep in my spirit I believe I will heal, My blood and my body are healing now."

CLAUDIA: . . . bathed in my blood . . .

BREANNA: "Abundant Life Forces flow in me, filling me with faith . . . "

CLAUDIA: . . . and I was in rapture.

BREANNA: "The Goddess force is in me and healing me now."

Silence. BREANNA is smeared with blood and powder, arms outstretched.

CLAUDIA: I was in rapture.

BLACKOUT

END OF PLAY

BIBLIO

by Wayne Peter Liebman

AUTHOR'S NOTE

Biblio was commissioned and produced by the Road Theatre Company in North Hollywood, January – February, 2007, as part of Cuts, an evening of short plays by DogEar. Anne Noble played Glynda, Mark Doerr played Parker, and Mara Marini played Marilyn. The play was directed by Dennis Gersten.

The playwrights were given two items on which to build their plays—a pair of scissors and the theme of duplicity. Biblio was further inspired by a chance encounter I had with a poem about a girl's search for her mysterious, absent father, which contained this line: *Because it is my nature to deceive you.*

The play spins out of control from there.

— Wayne Peter Liebman

CAST OF CHARACTERS

GLYNDA — 20s. Eggshell fragile.

PARKER — Glynda's dad. 50s.

MARILYN — 20s or 30s. Very blonde.

BIBLIO

A child's bedroom. London or somewhere. Glynda in bed or on a futon. Bedtime. Music, which begins in darkness—Sinatra: "Young at Heart" Glynda wears a child's nightgown. She is cutting out paper dolls with a scissors and taping them to a book.

GLYNDA: (*to audience*) This is my book. Glynda's book. In London. Or somewhere.

(*she becomes five*)

Daddy!

(*no answer*)

Dance with me, daddy!

Music changes to "Begin the Beguine." PARKER enters dancing with an imaginary partner. He is dressed elegantly, very James Bond. He wears a hat and dances wonderfully.

PARKER: It's bedtime, sweetie.

GLYNDA: Where's mommy?

PARKER: Asleep, baby. Like you should be.

GLYNDA: (*pouting*) The music's too loud. *(She gets out of bed and assumes a dance pose.)*

Just a little?

(He joins her. They dance. He carries her to bed. He kisses her goodnight.)

Put it in me, daddy.

(He doesn't respond, but gets up and dances offstage with his imaginary partner. Music fades. She speaks to the audience.)

He doesn't fuck me. He never fucks me. This never happened. I'm an unreliable narrator. Did you ever do it in a library? Christ, I need a smoke.

Crossfade to dim light.

She throws off the nightgown. Underneath she wears a long white blouse and, if we could see under that, which we can't, panties. She walks to a kitchen table, tries to light a cigarette, inhales smoke from the match and immediately has a coughing fit.

GLYNDA: Fuck. (*She stubs the unlit cigarette out. Music: a rhumba, faintly.*) *Glynda.* Go figure.

PARKER enters, dancing.

GLYNDA: His name is Parker. We're in Buenos Aires. I'm seventeen.

PARKER sees GLYNDA, stops dancing, kisses her on the forehead.

PARKER: Hi, baby. (*He sits with her.*)

GLYNDA: This isn't Buenos Aires, is it daddy?

PARKER: No, baby.

GLYNDA: Vienna?

PARKER: No baby.

GLYNDA sighs. A very big sigh. Music starts to fade.

GLYNDA: Tell me a story?

PARKER: Once there was a little girl and she had a daddy who loved her very much.

GLYNDA: I hate you daddy. I'm going to be a librarian.

PARKER: He took her everywhere.

GLYNDA: You never took me anywhere. (*She spits it out.*) *Parker.*

PARKER: In his heart.

pause

GLYNDA: What is it you do, daddy?

PARKER: You know I can't talk about that, sweetie.

GLYNDA: Government. Spy, right?

PARKER: That's right, sweetie.

Dance music: driving, tense, Latin, such as "Batucada" from O Nosso Amor. MARILYN enters in a sexy dress. She's a knockout.

She carries, perhaps, a small Enigma machine, a thick book, an evening dress, all of which she eventually deposits on the table. She has a lot of trouble with everything.

PARKER: Marilyn!

GLYNDA: (*you've got to be kidding*) Marilyn?

MARILYN removes PARKER'S hat and runs her fingers through his hair. PARKER and MARILYN kiss. It's a very sexy kiss. GLYNDA gets up from the table.

GLYNDA: Oh, please.

MARILYN tosses the gown to GLYNDA.

MARILYN: You'll catch your death.

GLYNDA: (*Regards the gown. Of Marilyn—*) Who is she, daddy?

MARILYN exits. PARKER puts on a headset, consults the book and begins typing. Dance music fades. Radio static. Old-fashioned tuning sounds. Morse code.

PARKER: What, baby?

GLYNDA: Never mind, Mr. 007. (*She considers the gown.*) I don't think I can get into this. (*To audience*) Turn around, please. (*She waits a moment as no one turns.*) Fuck you.

She turns upstage, removes her blouse, wiggles into the gown. The result is somewhat disheveled. PARKER notices.

PARKER: You look beautiful, baby.

GLYNDA: DID I SAY YOU COULD WATCH ME? GO! (*He freezes, looking hurt.*) Please, just go.

He leaves. She sits on the edge of the stage and speaks to the audience. Lights darken around her. Radio sounds fade.

GLYNDA: It's some code thing. He translated. CIA or NSA or LBJ. Whatever. He would just call. Then we'd pick up and go after him. Berlin. Tokyo. I think we went. I lose the thread. My mother. Well, now it gets serious. I'm rambling, aren't I? My mother isn't in this play. She was very beautiful. He loved her. I think he loved her. She left him. I think he had her killed. No. First she died of natural causes. No. First she left him. Then she died of natural causes. Then he had her killed. Fuck that. I'm making this up. Anyway, he sent postcards. I knew where he'd been. I was, what, twenty? I was old enough. I knew he had women. I didn't give a damn about his fucking women. I was old enough to know.

Crossfade. MARILYN enters. She has a nurse's cap on. She straightens things up. GLYNDA hears, but doesn't look.

GLYNDA: Mommy?

MARILYN: Not a chance, honey. Time for your medicine.

GLYNDA: Where's my dad?

MARILYN: Busy busy busy.

GLYNDA: What're you, his agent?

MARILYN: That's right. Your daddy is a poet. A rock star.

GLYNDA: You play dress up with him, don't you.

MARILYN: All the time. Your daddy is a hero.

GLYNDA: Whore. You play hide the salami with my dad?

MARILYN: Your daddy, little Glynda, is the goddamn savior of the free world. Without your daddy there would be no United States. Just remember that.

MARILYN produces a syringe and empties it into GLYNDA's neck. GLYNDA tries to fend MARILYN off, but it's already over.

GLYNDA: MY DADDY TAKES A PISS AND YOU DRINK IT! MY DADDY KILLED KENNEDY! MY daddy . . . (*She is asleep.*)

Sinatra: "Pennies from Heaven" – Nelson Riddle arrangement. MARILYN drags GLYNDA off stage. PARKER enters opposite. He dances alone to the music and speaks to the audience.

PARKER: Here's the thing. Ring a ding ding. (*Laughs. He's drunk.*) How shall I put it? We live in an age . . . of . . . deception? (*laughs more, barely containing himself*) Oh, shit. Sorry. Okay. Do you know what I really wanted to be? A priest. And I end up . . . what . . . the Manchurian candidate.(*beat*) Glynda was the only thing I ever loved. Not her mother. Not . . . any of them. Glynda. (*beat*) The female child must suffer a defeat. At the hands of her mother. Freud, right? Glynda . . . was . . . sort of rained out. (*A sigh. He stops dancing. Music stops.*) No joy in Mudville. (*beat*) Hey, how 'bout them Yankees!

Crossfade. GLYNDA enters dishabille. Attempts to smooth her hair and apply lipstick have failed.

GLYNDA: Daddy?

PARKER: Baby?

GLYNDA: Dance with me, daddy.

PARKER: Music's over, sweetie. Play's over.

GLYNDA: Dance anyway.

They dance real close. There is no music.

PARKER: I'm so tired, baby.

GLYNDA: I'm dreaming, aren't I daddy?

PARKER: I don't think so, baby.

GLYNDA: Hold me tight.

PARKER: Tight as night.

GLYNDA: Love you, daddy.

PARKER: Love you, baby.

They dance over to the futon (or bed) and lay down together. GLYNDA soothes him, kisses his face. He sleeps. The scissors from the first scene are still on the bed. GLYNDA fingers them. She is thinking of using them on PARKER. She is thinking about it very seriously. MARILYN enters.

MARILYN: Glynda? There you are. Come away now.

GLYNDA gets up and brandishes the scissors.

GLYNDA: Fuck off, (*spits it out*) Marilyn.

MARILYN: Time to wake up, dear. It's not healthy.

GLYNDA: I'm not sleeping.

(MARILYN takes a step toward GLYNDA.)

MARILYN: Give me the scissors, baby.

GLYNDA: Who the fuck are you?

MARILYN takes another step.

MARILYN: I'm the good fairy. Give me the scissors. You don't want to hurt yourself. (*GLYNDA slashes the air with the scissors. MARILYN reacts as if stabbed.*) Jesus, baby! (*She struggles to stand but can't. She lays down on the floor and then is still.*)

GLYNDA: Who the fuck are you!

Crossfade to dim light. GLYNDA drops the scissors. She retrieves the book from the bed, a string of cut dolls hanging out, and sits on the edge of the stage and addresses the audience. Lights close around her.

GlYNDA: I have this memory. He's in an easy chair reading a book. It's a big, heavy book. He doesn't want me to see what's in it. Codes? Girls? A bible? The funny thing is, I . . . need to think of the book. I can't . . . you know, do myself, without thinking of the book. I really do want to be a librarian. It's all I ever wanted.

Music: Louis Armstrong, "A Kiss to Build a Dream on." Radio static. Tuning. Morse code. Lights fade.

END OF PLAY

CHILLIN'

by Katy Hickman

AUTHOR'S NOTE

In the wake of 9/11, the White House press secretary warned citizens to "watch what they say, watch what they do." What do you do with that? At the very least, it was intended to get people to shut up. It also sounded like rules for a new oppressive game we were all being forced to play. I was drawn to the teens who play at war, and wondered how they might navigate the reality of the so-called "war on terror."

Chillin' was part of a weekend of staged readings of new plays from Dog Ear Playwrights called *Chatter*, presented at 24th Street Theatre as part of their *Intrigue, Lies, Secrets, and Spies* 2005 season. Aaron was played by A.J. Knox, Emil was played by Daniel Campagna, and the reading was directed by David P. Moore.

The use of italics is intended to disclose an aspect of the characters. Actors, interpret at will.

— Katy Hickman

CAST OF CHARACTERS

AARON — late teens, hefty-ish.

EMIL — Aaron's friend, late teens.

CHILLIN' BY KATY HICKMAN

A room in an American home in 2005. Two high school students, AARON and EMIL, are playing Dark Nathan, a video game that is like "Halo." AARON is slightly heftier than average. AARON's leg is in a makeshift cast as a result of a skate boarding accident. On a table in front of him are celery stalks, along with Doritos and pub cheese, or some other unhealthy snack items.

AARON: What about, like, being terrorists? *(feeling a twinge of pain)* I need to get some exercise. Doctor says I'm obese. *(stretches out his leg)*

EMIL: What about swimming?

AARON: Swimming's for old people. I find water to be creepy.

EMIL: You don't look obese. *(pause)* How fat do you have to be to be obese?

AARON: Not that fat, obviously. I'm not morbidly obese, just obese.

EMIL: I never think of guys being obese . . . Just ladies and children. I wonder if I'm obese . . . What did you say before?

AARON: When?

EMIL: Before.

AARON: I don't know. *(beat)*Isn't it weird that there aren't more attacks?

EMIL: What do you mean?

AARON: I mean, is it not weird that there aren't more attacks? Here?

EMIL: What kind of attacks?

AARON: Terrorist attacks. There aren't any.

EMIL: Well, no, if they're keeping *out* the ones that want to do it.

AARON: But isn't it weird that there haven't been *any* car bombs since Timothy McVeigh?

EMIL: I guess.

AARON: Not a single one here. That's just weird. *(beat)* Because car bombs are the easiest – I mean the easiest – kind of shit to put together.

EMIL: But Aaron, you're joking, right? What did you say before?

AARON: Before what?

EMIL: Before you told me you're obese.

AARON: I don't know. I'm just talking.

EMIL: You said something like we should be—you said something about terrorists.

AARON: I absolutely did not say that.

(*pause*)

AARON: Hey come on, E-mail. Play. What?

EMIL: Are you upset about something?

AARON: Upset? No. *Annoyed*.

EMIL: But, in a large way, you wouldn't ever, I mean, you don't hate anything, right?

AARON: Nah, nah, it's not that. It's like, the homeland is not getting a workout, know what I'm saying?

EMIL: A workout?

AARON: We're just like, tooling along on a raft. We're sitting here, but nothing's really happening. Psychologically, maybe, but not *actually*.

EMIL So you'd think about doing something so we'd be . . . better prepared?

AARON: Me? I wouldn't *do* anything . . .I'm just wondering what the terrorists are doing, that's all. I don't know, that's part of it; not just that. It's just so easy, is all. Like if you went to the water supply and poured something even harmless in, like Mountain Dew, like, but they thought it *was* something—that would just mess everything up. Or if you called, if you just called in threats, like ongoing, people would just freak and bunker it.

EMIL: (*resumes game*) We'll be fine, then. You're just bullshitting.

AARON: Yeah, come on, I'm just *thinking*. It's like preemptive thinking. If I *were* a terrorist, a little can of Dew could just screw everything up and make things all untenable and shit.

EMIL: What would that accomplish?

AARON: I don't think it would *accomplish* anything. And I wouldn't. I'm just talking, E-mail. Nothing you do accomplishes anything, anyway, unless earning money to buy paper to wipe your ass is accomplishing something. That's about the extent of it. Do you know anyone who really accomplishes anything?

EMIL: Dude, you need to stop calling me "E-mail."

AARON: Sorry, Emilio, but I ask you: who do you know who accomplishes anything.

EMIL: I know lots of people.

AARON: Name one.

EMIL: Bono.

AARON: Someone you know.

EMIL: My aunt is a teacher.

AARON: Good for her. But what does she accomplish, really? She teaches, what 35 kids? (*calculating*) Six hours a day, a hundred eighty days a year, that's 1,080 hours, out of 8,760 hours in a given year. So that's what, 12 percent of the year they're in school. The rest of the time, 88 percent—88 friggin' percent—they're with, you know (*blanks out*) What, your aunt is caring and gives them some vocabulary. Next?

EMIL: Never mind, asshole. Come on, I don't need this shit.

AARON: You don't have to be in my cell! (*beat*) It's a joke! Emil!

EMIL: You're creeping me out.

AARON: I'm sorry, man, I don't mean to. It should be comforting, what I'm saying, actually, because, like I said, *nothing's happening.*

EMIL: Yeah, it's super comforting.

AARON: Come on. Everybody thinks about it. Not just me. I'm not being *revelatory.* Something's not *working.* Because if I'm thinking about, you know, the water supply and stuff, that means other people are, too. Some people get arrested for just talking about stuff, and that's messed up. The Government's solution just makes people *think* about terrorists all the time, or think *like* them, because we're trying to be *vigilant* or whatever. But ultimately, it doesn't even matter if anything actually happens because *thinking* is just getting . . . *spoiled.* Preoccupation *itself* becomes the master, Emil. It doesn't matter if it's preoccupation with car bombs, or security, or ports; once you're totally consumed with, say, protecting the Port of San Pedro, it doesn't even matter what happens to it; the *obsession* becomes what you *live* for. It's like mass Munchausen Syndrome by Proxy.

(*pause*)

EMIL: I gotta go.

AARON: What are you going to call 1-800-terrorist and rat me out?

EMIL: No.

AARON: I haven't done anything. I'm just talking in an abstract way.

EMIL: I just have to go.

AARON: You don't ever think about this stuff?

EMIL: Aaron, I—no. I don't have to think about it; it's always there. I'm not going to make a choice to think about it more if I don't have to. That's what they probably want, anyway. So I'm not going to. Just stick to the rules.

AARON: The rules.

EMIL: My rules.

AARON: Ooo-kay. Me, too.

EMIL: Why are you being all mocky?

AARON: I'm not.

EMIL: Yeah, you're all mocky. I'm going.

AARON: But are you going to tell?

EMIL: Nah, nah.

AARON: You know, that's fine, Emil. Go ahead, I don't care. Really. What are they going to do? What am I going to do? I'm obese.

EMIL: Aaron, for sure, like in school if you started talking about having revenge or hated a teacher or something, I'd, you know, I'd say something.

AARON: Right on.

EMIL: You don't have any guns, do you?

AARON: Hell no! I don't have any guns. I don't have any revenge. I don't—come on! Why would I want to do anything? No one's teasing me. I'm not isolating; I'm sharing!

EMIL: I really have to go, I do.

AARON: A school is such a soft target though, don't you agree?

EMIL: Stop it!

AARON: But it's just weirdo American people who shoot at schools, not terrorists. So far, anyway. That's what's so *weird*, Emil! That's what creeps *me* out!

EMIL: Just stop thinking about it!

AARON: All these places; movie theatres, underground parking structures, museums, shit, none of these places is protected at all!

EMIL: They shouldn't be! They're not supposed to be! They're supposed to be open. Free.

AARON: I know, I think so, too! I agree! I'm just *noting*. (*beat*) God it's lonely just to think anymore. (*beat*) You said you had to go, so go already.

EMIL: Dude. You seem worried.

AARON: That's it, I'm just worried.

EMIL: Are you going to be okay?

AARON: Of course. I've got my celery and Dark Nathan. I'll text you. Where do you "have to go," anyway?

EMIL: I'm going to some movie with Jan. I told her I would. I'm late.

AARON: That's cute. Seeing a movie with your mom. Tell her hi for me.

EMIL: Okay.

AARON: Are you going to tell her what I said?

EMIL: Yeah I'll tell her. What. I'll tell her hi, is that what you meant?

AARON: If you decide you *need to talk*, Emil, just tell her everything, okay? Don't tell her just what *you* want to make yourself the center of some dramatic story, okay? Just don't leave anything out, just be fair.

EMIL: "Dramatic story?" You're the one into dramatic stories, Aaron. Don't put that shit on me. You really should go swimming or something.

AARON: But if you don't tell her everything, it won't really be the truth. That wouldn't be fair. I *do* care about *that*.

(*beat*)

EMIL: I can't remember everything.

AARON: Whatever.

(*a beat*)

EMIL: I'll just tell her you're obese.

AARON: Dude.

(*EMIL leaves. AARON tries to get comfortable and goes back to his video game.*)

AARON: I definitely need to get some exercise.

BLACKOUT

END OF PLAY

VOX STELLARUM

by Leon Martell

AUTHOR'S NOTE

Vox Stellarum was produced at the MET Theatre in Los Angeles, September— October, 2005 under the original title "Diana the Throat Singer", as part of Dog Ear Playwrights' *The Witching Hour*. When Wayne suggested we write witch plays I started writing a grotesque adventure but then I remembered something far more affecting that had actually happened to me. The play is based on that event, one of those unexplainable things that happen and leaves you pondering for the rest of your life. I still don't know what really happened and where she really went. When the play was performed at the MET, the role of Leonard was played by Bernie Zilinskas, the role of Diana was played by Jennifer Blake and it was directed by Alicia Wollerton. The play is also available in Audio form at: http://www.dogear.org/files/Vox.mp3

— Leon Martell

CAST OF CHARACTERS

LEONARD — A young actor, several years out of college and early in his career.

DIANA — A couple of years younger than Leonard with an otherworldly quality. A singer.

VOX STELLARUM

LEONARD, a moderately handsome young man, addresses the audience.

LEONARD: People ask me, "You're an actor. What's your closest brush with 'the big time'? The REALLY 'big time'?" They're not even aware that it's a minor insult because, by default, it's accepting that I am "small time", but I still try to be gracious and I usually surprise them. "Summer Stock" . . . returning to the old college town. An old acquaintance, a very attractive acquaintance, shows up, as a fan, and invites me to dinner.

A small intimate restaurant. LEONARD and a young woman sit at a table. She, DIANA, is beautiful in an ethereal way. They are staring into each other's eyes. After too long, the woman averts her eyes. The young man gasps like he's been under water to the point of near drowning.

LEONARD: What was that?

DIANA: I don't know. It's something I can do . . . with some people. I'm sorry. It may have gone on too long.

LEONARD: That was forty-five minutes! It was (*still gasping*) like my skin was taken off an all my insides were pulled out. It felt . . . not bad . . . just like I was being . . . like my data was being gone over.

DIANA: Yeah, that's how it feels, at least the first time.

LEONARD: I could see colored threads . . .

DIANA: Luminous fibers . . .

LEONARD: Yes! Coming out of my navel and going to you . . . and back in a loop.

DIANA: Yes.

LEONARD: You never did that when we were in college. What was that?

DIANA: Don't worry. It's safe. You could do it. It's just training. I can't really even do it yet. I just have the basics.

LEONARD: When did you start? What IS that?

DIANA: It's from singing. I don't know if you remember . . .

LEONARD: Right. You were a singer . . .

DIANA: I'm not all that good . . .

LEONARD: You were good, but I don't remember fibers.

DIANA: I hadn't experienced the throat singing.

LEONARD: Is that . . . they make a couple of different pitches at the same time . . .

DIANA: Yes! Parallel resonances. There's a group of throat singers in Portland.

LEONARD: What are they doing in Portland?

DIANA: Singing. I went to a recital and I was just shaken and after one of them came right through the crowd to me and said, "Come sing," and I did. I quit teaching elementary school. I just studied with the throat singers.

She freezes. He addresses the audience.

LEONARD: Fuck me, I'm on a date with a space alien. Diana is a space alien! Or maybe this isn't her. Maybe it's like the pod people, she's been taken over by a space alien. What the fuck!? I didn't know her that well before, but . . . I would have noticed if she was pulling out people's fibers. I would have heard about it if she . . .

She unfreezes and he instantly returns his focus to her.

DIANA: Of course, Tommy doesn't understand any of this . . .

She freezes and he turns to the audience.

LEONARD: Right! I'm on a date with a married space alien. Fuck!

He turns back to her reality. She unfreezes.

DIANA: So, I'm back here visiting Mom and Dad, they don't understand, and I saw your picture in the paper. "Local actor returns to play Feste in *Twelfth Night*."

She freezes. He addresses the audience again.

LEONARD: I should have gone to West Virginia and done *The Hobbit*. No, I wanted to do Shakespeare. Of course I had to play Feste, the "fool". *(Gasp)* Maybe she hears all this!

He returns his attention to her. She unfreezes.

LEONARD: And . . . When you . . . did that to me. What did you see? Can you tell what I'm thinking?

DIANA: *(laughing)* No. It's not like that. It's a different language. Like a spectrum.

LEONARD: And?

DIANA: It's not "words". It's more like . . . music. I can see your music.

LEONARD: What kind of music am I? Am I a Polka or something?

DIANA: You're . . . a good man. *(Seductively)* Let's go to the cornfield.

He starts to quibble. She waves her hand in an elegant gesture and they are in transit. She might also sing quietly, something beautiful and exotic. He talks to the audience.

LEONARD: She must mean her parents' cornfield. They're from here. Old New England family. Way old. Pilgrims old. Witch trials, curses, Indian massacres old . . . from when spirits walked these woods. Things that were driven out when they cut down the old growth. Forest things . . . that are angry . . .

With a gesture from her, they have arrived. They stand in the middle of the corn. The sounds of a summer night. The rustling of the corn.

DIANA: It's perfect, isn't it? Look at the stars.

LEONARD: I forgot about them. In the city you don't even see them.

DIANA: They are all radiating, vibrating at individual frequencies. Sending it out toward us. Not really toward "us", but we are part of where it reaches.

He talks to the audience.

LEONARD: This is where the spaceship descends.

Back to her reality.

DIANA: And the corn. Listen. The wind strokes each stalk into vibration. Plucks it like a harp. We are in the middle of a chord being played. As the corn grows the pitch changes and the whole field sends out its message. Can you hear the trees beyond? Oak. Maple. Pines. *(Turning to him.)* Let's join them. Give me your hand.

LEONARD: Alright.

DIANA: Here, touch me.

She puts his hand in the center of her chest and puts her own hand in the center of his. She sings.

DIANA: Feel the vibration?

LEONARD: Yeah.

DIANA: With me.

LEONARD: What?

She sings.

DIANA: Send your vibrations into my hand.

He sings with her.

DIANA: Good! Don't hold back. Let everything go. Release everything.

They sing together. The sound rises. Other tones join them. It reaches a peak and stops. He gasps.

LEONARD: That was amazing!

DIANA: You could come with me.

LEONARD: Where? As what? Are we . . . lovers? What about your husband?

DIANA: He doesn't understand. You have a gift. I saw it in your singing.

LEONARD: In the play?

DIANA: That's when I knew you could make the leap.

LEONARD: Those songs in the play, they're just little ditties . . .

DIANA: And the madrigals. You always loved madrigals.

LEONARD: Oh, I'm not a real singer . . .

DIANA: You just need to study, with the right teachers, and it's even better if you have someone to study with.

LEONARD: I would really love to, but, I have another job waiting for me in the city as soon as the summer's done.

DIANA: In college, when you played Biff in "The Death of a Salesman", I was doing props and you came off stage and said, "For a minute, I left the ground."

LEONARD: I was a pompous little shit.

DIANA: No! This is a chance to leave the ground.

LEONARD: I . . I can't. I'm just lucky to have another job. Acting. Right away. It's with a very respected director. We're doing *Death Trap*.

DIANA: It's alright. It was just an offer. I don't know why I thought you'd want to come. It's not for everyone.

They kiss.

DIANA: Goodbye.

She exits.

LEONARD: I saw her once again, maybe a year later. She came to a play I was doing with a dark man in white robes. She was beautiful and wished me well. Then she disappeared. Not in a puff of smoke but after that time, I couldn't find her. I tried all the old places, all the old numbers, her parents, he ex-husband . . . She just wasn't on the same plane of existence anymore. I'm still acting. T.V. sometimes. I'm usually over the shoulder of the lead detective saying, "I'll call homicide," that kind of thing. It makes my family happy. "Look, he's an actor! He's on T.V.!" I don't do musicals. The last time I sang on stage was that summer. "Twelfth Night." Most people play it like a broad comedy because that's what the summer stock audiences want, but it's dark. Everybody gets married, blah blah blah . . . but in the end it's Feste, the fool, alone on stage.

He sings.

LEONARD:

When that I was and a little tiny boy

With a hey, ho, the wind and the rain,

A foolish thing was but a toy,

For the rain it raineth every day.

With a hey, ho, the wind and the rain,

The rain it raineth every day.

Lights fade out.

END OF PLAY.

BEAUTIFUL

by Jacqueline Wright

AUTHOR'S NOTE

I had the pure joy of creating *Beautiful* for the Virginia Ave Project, a non-profit organization that works with at risk kids, pairing them with playwrights and other theatre artists to create an evening of plays.

I had been wanting to write a play or poem to express my love and gratitude for my grandmother while also honoring our authentic relationship. She and I were, in many ways, very different people with different political views and different views of God—but that difference always led to exciting conversations and inspired a desire to understand—not necessarily agree with—each other's point of view.

I wrote *Beautiful* with my grandmother tucked away in my heart, allowing real moments between us to expand into taller tales. Telling "tall tales" and getting in trouble for this as children was one thing my grandma and I both had in common. When she was five she told her friends at school that her father had found gold on their property "way down deep." The story spread and pretty soon neighbors from miles around were riding their horse drawn buggies up to the house to see the gold, leaving her daddy to clear up the mess.

The title was inspired by another grandmother—a neighbor of

mine. Her seven year-old grandson would introduce her as "my Beautiful." And she would beam every time. Just like my own grandmother did when she saw the play for the first time. She passed away two years ago. And this little play still speaks my heart as truly as the day I wrote it. It is dedicated to Mildred Neil West. To Beautiful. And to all Grandmothers.

Special thanks to the Virginia Ave Project and Theatre of NOTE for producing the play, to Dan Bonnell for direction, and to all the actors who have played Beautiful and Tasha.

Original cast from Virginia Ave and Theatre of Note:

Beautiful : Kebe Dunn, Lynn O'dell

Tasha: Mckenzie Graves and Mandi Moss

— Jacqueline Wright

CAST OF CHARACTERS

TASHA — a 12-16 year-old-girl, wrestling with her grandmother's mortality (any ethnicity).

BEAUTIFUL — Tasha's grandmother, 60-120 (any ethnicity).

BEAUTIFUL

BEAUTIFUL'S room. TASHA, a 14-year-old girl, is looking up at the stars in the sky. BEAUTIFUL, her grandmother, lies in bed. TASHA addresses the audience.

TASHA: Beautiful died. She called me into her room, we were all lined up to say our good-byes at her door. I was the last one. I didn't want to go in. I didn't want to say goodbye. I prefer hellos.

She pauses.

I wanted to be strong. I wanted to be generous. I wanted to be anything except what I was.

TASHA crosses to her grandmother.

Hello, Beautiful.

BEAUTIFUL: Hello, Tasha.

TASHA: *(addressing the audience)* She called my brother Flight and my mother Gentle Flower. Me– she just called me my real name, Tasha. That always bothered me.

BEAUTIFUL: Sit.

TASHA sits.

BEAUTIFUL: How was your day today?

TASHA: Fine.

BEAUTIFUL: Anything new?

TASHA: The same as any day.

Slight pause.

BEAUTIFUL: Why won't you look at me?

Slight pause.

BEAUTIFUL: Do you fear you'll catch death from Beautiful?

TASHA: No.

BEAUTIFUL: Perhaps I will catch life from you.

TASHA tries to look at BEAUTIFUL.

TASHA: I can't.

BEAUTIFUL: Are you afraid?

Tasha *shakes her head "no."*

BEAUTIFUL: Sad–

TASHA shakes her head "no."

BEAUTIFUL: We've never kept secrets between us, have we?

TASHA: No.

BEAUTIFUL: Even when we don't see things the same way. When you painted your room lilac and you asked if I thought it was beautiful– what did I say?

TASHA: That you hated lilac. You thought it was a weak color and it made you queasy.

Tasha *laughs.*

BEAUTIFUL: Why are you laughing?

TASHA: I–just, you always have such . . . dramatic feelings, even about the color of a room!

BEAUTIFUL: You were angry with me. You told me, lilac was beautiful and it made you giddy and unlike me, hungry, not queasy. And did I get angry?

TASHA: No. You said you'd finally have to face your fear of lilac–

BEAUTIFUL: And I sat in your room and breathed it all in. And me and lilac got on fine with each other ever since.

TASHA: You're so weird.

BEAUTIFUL: It's the Indian in me.

TASHA: You're not Indian. You make up tall tales–

BEAUTIFUL: I'm Indian in my heart. A warrior. And therefore, I am Indian.

TASHA: OK.

BEAUTIFUL: No secrets.

Slight pause.

TASHA: I'm angry.

BEAUTIFUL: Angry at me?

TASHA: Yes.

BEAUTIFUL: Let us not part with secrets.

TASHA: I'm angry that you're going. I'm mad cuz you seem like you're not even fighting– like you lied about your warrior heart! And I hate to see you weak and not able to pick flowers with me and I'm so mad that you won't be here when I paint my room yellow or green and I won't know all the ways color can make you feel and who am I going to tell my secrets to? And our word, authentic, will be lost and when I feel different than everyone else, I will have no one to share with and I only like the way you make my eggs, fried so hard they bounce and I think you've given up the fight, with no regard to me!

Image: An unbelievably large moon, half hidden by a purple hill.

TASHA: And I keep thinking about that day when we saw the moon. It was so huge– remember– it was gigantic and we thought–

BEAUTIFUL: There is no way that could be the moon–

TASHA: We thought it was a sign or a light or a spaceship. We got in the car and followed it, we went up that steep hill both looking up at that giant orb, until we saw it plain as day– the moon, floating in the sky.

Image: The giant moon in the sky.

BEAUTIFUL: I'd never seen a moon like that–

TASHA: No one will chase the moon with me. Be willing to drive all night– except you.

BEAUTIFUL: You may be right.

TASHA: Life won't be the same. I can't imagine a day without you.

BEAUTIFUL: Nor can I.

Pause.

TASHA: And don't tell me you'll be here in my heart or in a sunset or how I can talk to you whenever I want, in my prayers.

BEAUTIFUL: I won't.

TASHA: Or that you're going to heaven and one day we'll meet up there.

BEAUTIFUL: OK.

TASHA: Just admit– you're leaving.

Slight pause.

BEAUTIFUL: I'm leaving.

Pause.

TASHA: Why?

BEAUTIFUL: It's time for me to go.

TASHA: Why?

BEAUTIFUL: I don't know. It's just time.

TASHA: And you call yourself a warrior?

BEAUTIFUL: A warrior is different than a fighter.

TASHA: No it's not—a warrior fights.

BEAUTIFUL: A warrior faces challenges with dignity and a straight back. She faces all that stands before her.

TASHA: And what stands before you, Beautiful?

BEAUTIFUL: The unknown. The same unknown you also face.

TASHA: Days without you.

BEAUTIFUL: Yes.

TASHA: I hate the unknown.

BEAUTIFUL: I love the unknown.

TAHSA: Why?

BEAUTIFUL: I love surprises.

Slight pause.

BEAUTIFUL: Hand me my walking stick.

TASHA picks up BEAUTIFUL'S walking stick.

TASHA: You painted it lilac.

BEAUTIFUL: Terrible color.

TASHA hands her the walking stick.

TASHA: You do know this is 2016. People don't climb up a hill in the suburbs to die.

BEAUTIFUL: I'm not people. I'm Beautiful.

BEAUTIFUL sits up.

TASHA: Aren't you afraid?

BEAUTIFUL: Sure.

BEAUTIFUL stands, using her walking stick for balance.

TASHA: You're just gonna sit up there until you die?

BEAUTIFUL: I want to die, under the sun and then the stars. Look out and think of you and Flight and Gentle Flower and say hello, to Unknown.

TASHA: How come you never gave me a name?

BEAUTIFUL: Because I knew one day you would carry my name.

BEAUTIFUL opens the door, she looks back at TASHA.

BEAUTIFUL: Goodbye, Beautiful.

BEAUTIFUL walks out the door. TASHA watches her leave. She turns and addresses the audience.

TASHA: She climbed up the steep green hill, which we could see from our backyard. She stood, with her back straight, her thick black hair blowing in the wind.

Image: BEAUTIFUL, standing on the top of a hill, back straight, hair blowing in the wind. Her walking stick in her hand.

We all woke up early, on the 3rd day. The sun was breaking through the clouds and we all knew she had gone.

Image: The steep hill at sunrise. BEAUTIFUL is gone.

We hiked up the hill and there she was, sitting up, cross-legged like an Indian. Her lilac walking stick, firmly planted in the ground. Each of us saw a gift, a surprise she had left behind. A handful of poppy seeds for my mother, Gentle Flower. The wing of a crow for my brother, Flight. And a lilac-colored walking stick, with my name engraved, Beautiful. There is no one like my Beautiful. No one that has such great words and feeling about the color of my room, now moon-yellow. My mom says "It looks nice." My brother says "Uh, huh." I think of what she would say– I never asked her about moon-yellow. And I don't know where she is and I don't talk to her much, cuz I don't want to put words in her mouth that aren't hers. I think what I think, is this: I want to carry Beautiful inside of me, for the people I meet. For my future grandchildren. And for myself. I carry our word, authentic, in my pocket. And when I feel like the odd one out, I roll this word, between my thumb and finger.

(She retrieves BEAUTIFUL'S walking stick and sits on BEAUTIFUL'S bed.)

Someday, when I face the big unknown, I will pass my name and walking stick on to someone I love, perhaps a grand-daughter, but the color of the walking stick, will not be lilac– it will be her color, maybe something awful, like orange, which smells like marmalade and makes my lips pucker.

Lights fade out.

END OF PLAY

.

ABOUT THE PLAYWRIGHTS

KIM DUNBAR (*1331*):

Kim Dunbar was born in Los Angeles, and studied theater at U.C. San Diego and The Juilliard School. Her play *Porchmonkey* was first runner-up for NRT's National Play Award. Her other plays include *Taco Mundo*, *The Giver*, and *Banned and Burned in America*, (co-written with Bryan Davidson). Kim's plays have been developed/produced by Watts Village Theater Company, River Stage, Mark Taper New Work Festival, The Working Theater, Black Theater Artist's Workshop, ASK Theater Labs, Crossroads Theater, Greenway Court Theater, and the Black & Latino Playwright's Conference in San Marcos, Texas. Kim most recently wrote the book for the musical stage play *Mahalia's World: Remembering Mahalia Jackson*, and has also written several plays for young people though the Virginia Avenue Project. Kim will be working next with Los Angeles high school students and the RFK Center for Justice & Human Rights, at their Speak Truth to Power summer institute program.

.

ROBERT FIELDSTEEL (*Essential Magick*):

Robert Fieldsteel's plays have been produced in Los Angeles,

New York and Chicago. For *Crazy Drunk*, he received the L.A. Drama Critics Circle Award for Best World Premiere Play and the *Backstage West* Garland Award for Playwriting. Other works include *Smart* (N.Y. & Chicago productions, Trustus Festival and Pillars Prize finalist), his adaptation (with Jennifer Maisel and April Vanoff) of Ansky's *The Dybbuk* (5 L.A. Weekly Award Nominations), *Asylum* (O'Neill finalist*), Essential Magick* (Actors Theatre of Louisville Heideman Award finalist), and several youth theatre pieces for the Virginia Avenue Project.

Also an L.A. Drama Critics Circle Award-winning actor, he has guest starred frequently on television and acted in films for such directors as John Cassavetes and Sidney Lumet.

He currently lives, writes and teaches in Macon, GA, where he is Artist-in-Residence, Playwriting at Wesleyan College. He is still a proud and active member of Dog Ear.

.

KATY HICKMAN (*Chillin'*):

Katy Hickman is an actor and playwright living in Los Angeles. Her play, *Bright Boy: The Passion of Robert McNamara* premiered at the Electric Lodge in an Ensemble Studio Theatre Los Angeles production. *Meteor Girl* (Dramalogue Awards for performance and writing, Bay Area Critics Circle Award) was developed at the Zspace Studio for San Francisco's Solo Mio Festival and went on to successful productions at the Encore Theatre and Magic Theatre in San Francisco, and at Theater Theatre and HBO Workspace in Los Angeles. Her play, *Nomenclature* was part of an evening, *Cuts,* at the Road Theatre. *Chillin',* was featured as part of 24th Street Theatre's season of Intrigue, Lies, Secrets and Spies. Other works include *Layered*

Bob, at the Met Theatre, *Open Enrollment,* produced in San Francisco as part of the Abydos Director's Festival; *Lucky* and *What I Did for Art,* for the Virginia Avenue Project.

.

WAYNE PETER LIEBMAN (*Biblio*):

Wayne Peter Liebman is a poet and playwright. His plays include *Better Angels* (Trustus Playwright's Prize), *Transference* (2004 National Playwrights Conference, O'Neill Theater Center; Maxim Mazumdar Prize). Other full-length work includes *Brimful of Push* (2nd place, Sprenger Lang Foundation's U.S. History Play Competition) and *The Sun Maiden* (EdgeFest/LA History Project presentation at the Autry National Museum).

Wayne is the author of *Tending the Fire* (Ally Press) and co-edited an anthology of poems, *Raising the Roof* (Bombshelter), for Habitat for Humanity. His poetry and prose are widely published and have been anthologized in *In the Company of Others* (Tarcher), *Beyond the Valley of the Contemporary Poets* (Sacred Beverage), and *Primary Care* (University of Iowa Press). His poetry was nominated for a Pushcart Prize in 2001. Under the pen name of Wolf Pascoe, he's the author of *Breathing for Two,* and the blog, *Just Add Father.*

.

JENNIFER MAISEL (*Goody Fucking Two Shoes*):

Jennifer Maisel's Pen West Literary Award finalist *There or Here* was workshopped at PlayPenn before its critically acclaimed run at New York's Hypothetical Theatre and is in talks for a London premiere. Her *The Last Seder* premiered Off-Broadway after productions in Chicago, D.C. and Los Angeles. Plays include *Goody Fucking Two Shoes* (ATL's Humana Festival), *birds* (Rorschach Theatre), *Eden* (Theatre of NOTE, Original Works Publishing), *Match* (Berkshire Playwrights Lab). Awards: Kennedy Center's Fund for New American Plays, Charlotte Woolard and Roger L. Stevens Awards; the 2014 Stanley Award for Drama; SCR's California Playwrights Competition; two time PEN West Literary Award finalist; five time Heideman Award finalist; STAGES International finalist. Jennifer received an Ensemble Studio Theatre/ Alfred P. Sloan foundation commission for *Out of Orbit*, developed at the Sundance Theatre Lab and the Gulf Shore New Play Festival. Her newest play, @thespeedofJake, has been twice honored by The Kilroys. She also writes for film and television. (wwwjennifermaisel.com)

.

LEON MARTELL (*Vox Stellarum*):

An MFA from the University of Iowa, Leon Martell co-founded the "Duck's Breath Mystery Theater" which has performed on stage, for N.P.R. and PBS.

As a member of Sam Shepard's writing workshop, he wrote the award winning "Hoss Drawin". At the Padua Hills Festival in Los Angeles, he participated as a writer, actor and director for thirteen years. His plays include "Kindling", "1961 El Dorado" co-written with wife Elizabeth Ruscio, "Mooncalf", "Feed Them Dogs", and "Hard Hat Area". His play with music, "STEEL – John Henry and the Shaker", received seven Ovation Award nominations, including "Best New Musical". His "Bea[u]tiful in the Extreme" is published by Original Works Publishing. Since 2006 he has been a writer for the Los Angeles Philharmonic's

Youth Concert Series, and the "Summer Sounds" Series at the Hollywood Bowl. He has been a writing instructor at UCLA Extension continuously since 1994.

.

STEVE TOTLAND (*Face Value*) :

Steve Totland is a playwright, performer, and teacher. He is a founding member of Lifeline Theatre (Chicago), where he worked on more than thirty productions during the company's first fifteen years.

His plays have been produced by Steppenwolf Theatre, Lifeline Theatre, the Road Theatre, 24th Street Theatre, The Virginia Avenue Project, stageworks/Hudson, Another Country Productions, the Herring Run Theatre Festival, and the Festival of New American Plays (London, England). His play You Are Here was finalist for the Ashland New Play Competition, and winner of the New Play Competition at Center Stage (Greenville, SC).

Steve earned his Ph.D. in Performance Studies at Northwestern University. He has taught classes in performance and playwriting at Northwestern University, University of Chicago, Pomona College, and The California Institute of the Arts. He is a member of DogEar, a playwright's collective, and the Dramatists Guild. Steve teaches theatre at The Buckley School in Los Angeles.

.

JACQUELINE WRIGHT (*Beautiful*):

Jacqueline's mother was an airline stewardess and her father, first a navy pilot and later a newspaper publisher. Her first published story was in her father's newspaper at age 12; how to make jewelry out of tics. Her love of storytelling and adventure lead her to Cal Arts where she majored in theatre. She has received Ovation, LA Weekly and LA Drama Critics Circle nominations for acting and playwriting and two LA weekly awards for portraying JonBenet Ramsey in *House of Gold* and Clytemnestra in *Clyt at Home*. Her most recent play, *Have You Seen Alice*, received a critically acclaimed production at Theatre of Note. *Eat Me*, an early play of hers, produced in 2005, received six LA Weekly nominations, including best play. The feature film adaptation of *Eat Me* is currently in post production. For information about her plays visit www.dogear.org.

ACKNOWLEDGMENTS

Cover art: *The Sun at His Eastern Gate*, Watercolor Illustration to Milton's L'Allegro and Il Penseroso by William Blake.

Book and cover design: Wayne Peter Liebman